GOOD NEWS

How Jesus Turns Every Minus Into a Plus

JACOB COYNE

Foreword by Jarrid Wilson

Only Good News

Copyright © 2019 by Jacob Coyne

All rights reserved. No part of this book may be reproduced or transmitted in any form or by any means without written permission from the author.

ISBN (9781718078888)

Printed in USA.

Jacobcoyne.com

ONLY GOOD NEWS

DEDICATION

Mariah, the woman of my dreams, my best friend. You show me the beauty of Jesus every day. You've made me the happiest man on the earth, and I'll spend the rest of my life trying to return the favor. Thank you for calling out the best in me. Thank you for raising our kids in such a deep love.

Mom and Dad. You raised Jonah and I in a home where Jesus was present. You loved us so well. Dad, I'll never forget the night at Eldon's where Jonah and I were born-again.

Greg. Thanks for all the laughter, the lessons, and the love you blessed me with. I'll see you in heaven one day.

Jonah. God is too good to me to give me a brother like you. I love you and believe in you, always. You're my hero.

Tyler and Amber. You love so well. You've changed my life more than you know. Thank you for showing me what it looks like to give Jesus everything. You are solid gold. I'll always cherish the Sollies and look up to you both.

Chris O. Your faith moves mountains, and your faith in me and has moved me as well. Thank you for believing in me and calling me into God's promises and plan. America shall be saved!

My girls. My gifts from above. My heart is full. I'll always be there for you, and I promise to protect you, cheer you on, and show you Jesus the best way I know how.

ACKNOWLEDGEMENTS

A special thanks to all who supported this project!

Gail Spooner, Becke Rogers, Mom, Adam Barta, David Barta, Mike & Lori Salley, Chase Woodall, Jennifer Cullinane, Michael Brazil, Shane Winnings, Alexis Coyne, Jonah Coyne, Mike Root, Erin Freeman, Kailey Phillips, Jason Morse, Ashley Berg, Levi Hug, Luke Sankey, Matt Wakefield, Robert Davis, Christopher Davis, Jonathan Hernandez, Justin and Cara Bowen, Sarah Wind, Teresa McNeese, Daniel Newton, Jen Goeking, Brad Bodeman, Cindy Pierson, Tina Morton, Ryan Jordan, and Jeff Mattheis , Marda Stancil, Carol Kreuger, Jordan Mast, Lonnetta Cunningham, … thank you a million times. Enjoy!

TABLE OF CONTENTS

Foreword   9

Welcome   12

The Lost   24

The Least   43

The Lifeless   55

The Last   91

The Little   103

About the Author   115

FOREWORD

Jarrid Wilson

Some of the best news I ever received in life was when my wife told me we were pregnant with our first child, Finch. I remember getting a call from my wife, Juli letting me know I needed to leave the office and get home as quickly as I could. She didn't give me any details other than that she wasn't injured.

I left my office as quickly as I could, probably driving a lot faster than I was legally supposed to. *What could it be?* I thought to myself. I really had no clue.

I arrived to the house in under 10 minutes, and I could tell that even she was impressed at how quickly I had made it home. *Are you okay?* I asked in a panic. She told me everything was fine, but that she had really important news to share with me.

She then proceeded to hold up a shirt that said 'Your going to be a daddy!' I remember being a utter shock, jumping up and down and yelling *Yes! Yes!*. It was some of the greatest news I had ever received in my entire life, and I know many other parents around the world would probably agree. Becoming a parent is unlike anything else in this world. It was the good news I had always dreamed of receiving one day.

But as incredible as that news was, there's actually something even more incredible in the world. Crazy. Right!?

Yup. It's the Good News of Jesus.

It's unlike anything else in the world, and it provides a hope and assurance that is incomparable. It's the Good News that keeps on giving, revealing, healing, encouraging, and molding us into the people God has called us to be.

This news isn't just the Good News, it's the greatest news the world has ever seen. Why? Because no matter how broken, messed up or unworthy of this news you think you are, this Good News is still available for you. It's available for everything. It's the antidote for a broken and hurting world.

From Genesis to Revelation, the Good News exudes from each and every page. It is the foundation in which we should build our lives upon, and the blueprint in which we should follow.

Like the news of me learning I was going to be a father, I found excitement, joy, and purpose that was unmatched. The Good News is Jesus will do that and then some. It will never return void. It's a river that won't run dry.

In his book, *Only Good News,* Jacob continually points the reader to the message and power of Jesus, never straying away from the truth that is found within The Gospel. This is a book you will not want to put down. In fact, you'll want to read it over and over again.

WELCOME

Has there ever been news that changed your entire life the moment you heard it? Maybe it was 9/11 or a death of a loved one. Maybe it was the job promotion you and your family were praying for. Maybe it was the the first time your significant other said "I love you too." Mine happened two years ago, when my wife surprised me with the news that we were having a baby! If you are a parent, you know that this news changes everything. There is a new person coming to the world that you are completely responsible for! There are so many things I had to let go of and sacrifice, and so many new things that I had to gain as a Dad. My wife, Mariah and I had nine months to prepare for one of the biggest days of our lives. Our daughter, River Jordan certainly did change everything. All of the sacrifices we made for her have become so easy, because we would never want to go back to our lives without her. There were so many friends and family members that would chime in with great advice for parenting during that time, which we were thankful for, but no advice could produce the love that began to grow in my heart the moment I heard the news about my daughter being conceived.

News changes everything.

When Jesus walked the earth, He came as a living, breathing announcement, declaring to the world the goodness of God through his life, death, and resurrection.

He didn't come to offer us good advice to live the perfect Christian life, He came bearing good news. The good news of Jesus isn't a list of do's and don'ts, it's not a message that will make us better people, it's an announcement that offers us all a new and abundant life. Good advice and formulas will tell us what needs to be done, but the Good News of Jesus tells us what already *has* been done. The good news changes everything. So in the next few chapters, we are going to find out what this good news is all about, and what actually has been accomplished for us all. Let me tell you a little bit of my story, and about how I desperately need the good news to invade my religious lifestyle of good formulas.

I remember the first time I prayed to Jesus at age five. I was being babysat by my grandma, and I was watching my local pastor, Fulton Buntain on TV. I asked my grandma if the man I was watching on the television was God, and she chuckled and told me about the real Jesus. My grandma lead me through a prayer that day to invite Jesus to live inside my heart. I'm not going to lie, I was always a little creeped out when I imagined a miniature Jesus actually living inside my five year old heart. Years went by and as I approached my teenage years, church became a chore and I lost interest in the whole religion thing. In my freshman and sophomore year at Curtis high school, my friends started to make fun of the fact that I was a 'good kid.' It seemed like every day at lunch, someone would mention the fact that "Jacob's still a virgin." or "Jacob doesn't drink," and "Jacob would never do that." I gave into the pressure like most teens do, and dove straight into a wild lifestyle of partying, smoking, drinking, and theft. Shame hit me hard, I mean really hard. I was too embarrassed to show my face at church, because I thought only the "really holy" people go there. Some Saturday nights I would arrive home still high from the weed I smoked at the party up the street, and I'd sneak into my room before my parents could smell my clothes, and pray to Jesus. I used to say "Jesus, I know you see what I'm doing, everyone else in school is doing it too. I promise I'll be a good Christian when I get married and have kids one day, but not now, I'm sure you understand.. I love you, amen." This prayer is comical, because that's obviously not how God works, and He had a different plan for me.

God didn't want to wait around and watch me waste my teenage years and 20's on myself. This wandering teenager was about to have an awakening. One day my dad came home from a men's Bible study group. I can remember this night so vividly. As I was playing Call of Duty on the Xbox, my dad walked into the dimly lit man cave and looked at my brother and I with the biggest smile and glow on his face. There was something new about him, something different. He had life in his eyes that I had never seen before. For some reason, when I looked at my dad I wanted to laugh and cry all at the same time. Dad told me that Jesus "set him free" and that he had "become a new man". I had grown up in a Christian home, attended church every weekend, but I had rarely seen anyone look the way my dad did that night. Jesus really did change him. This was real. This was God. I was more than convinced that I needed to be at this men's group the following Monday night. "What really happened to dad? Could Jesus change me?" At this point, I strongly believed that God wanted nothing to do with me. I had thoughts like, "How could God ever want to love someone who has hurt so many people?" "I am unlovable, and unforgivable, I'm a rebel and a mess." But seeing my dad so changed gave me a glimmer of hope. Maybe Jesus could give me another chance. Literally, the moment I walked into the home where the men's group took place, I began to weep in front of a bunch of grown men. It's as if I knew my life would change forever that night, and I could never go back. Once you know Jesus is real, how could you run from that truth? As the night went on, I became more and more eager to ask someone to pray over me the way they had prayed over my dad the week before. Finally, it was my turn and Eldon, the leader of the group, put his hand on my shoulder and asked me how he could pray for me. I told him I wanted what my dad had, so he prayed. Depression, shame, pain, and sadness left me all at once. I couldn't believe it! How could Jesus do this to someone like me? Tears then flooded my face as I physically felt the love of God saturate my soul. From my head to my feet, I felt the presence of Jesus flow through me. Then I couldn't believe what happened next, a different language started coming out of my mouth that I had never heard before. The men in the meeting explained to me that I was being set free and baptized in the Holy Spirit. (If you want a biblical reference to what happened to me, please see Acts chapter 2).

I was a new man. I left my past behind and had a new passion: Jesus, only Jesus. My heart burned for God day and night and all I wanted to do was serve Him. I stopped the partying, and all of the other crazy things I was doing at the time so I could make it to church as much as I could. There were some Sundays where I would church hop to 3 venues before the day was over.

All I wanted to do was be where Jesus followers were and worship Him. During school I would talk about Jesus and pray for my friends during class and at lunch. My favorite story about God moving through me in school was when a student on the football team ran up to me during pottery class screaming in pain because he hurt his knee. He asked me for prayer. I thought he was joking like some other peers did about my new faith in Jesus, so I jokingly punched his knee! He screamed even louder and his face got bright red. "Why'd you do that? My knee hurts even worse now!" I was in big trouble. I was beginning to think my face was going to hurt worse than his knee in a second. I told him I was sorry and I would love to pray for his knee. He hurt it the night before during football practice, then during class, he bumped into a door and hurt it worse, and then of course I punched it. I put my hand on his knee and prayed a quick 10 second prayer, and he jumped back in amazement. He said, "Bro, I wish I was lying to you, but God healed me when you prayed. All the pain is gone!" All throughout the rest of the week I heard him telling people about what God did. You'd think that things get better and better from here in my story, but as I did more for God in the next couple of years, my heart grew cold, callous, and desperate for answers.

Every time I showed up at the men's group where I met Jesus, they would ask my brother and I if we had any good testimonies of things God did through us the previous week. As weeks went by, a self imposed pressure grew in me to perform for them and for Jesus. The joy of seeing people touched by God left me, and now it was beginning to feel like a job, and if I didn't pray for anyone or lead anyone to Jesus that week, I felt like a failure and sinner. One week, I hadn't seen anything noteworthy, so I became desperate to see God work a miracle in a stranger's life. During this particular week in my senior year of high school, I had literally prayed for and witnessed to over 20 people with no results. It was the weekend now, and the Monday men's group was fast approaching, so I needed a miracle to bring to the group. My brother Jonah and I decided to go to Walmart at night and stay there until someone got healed by God or gave their life to Jesus, because hey, Walmart is open 24 hours! Within the first hour, my brother Jonah and I were able to lead a small group of teens to accept Jesus. This is the way I lived every day for the first few years of following Jesus.

I thought I was following Jesus, but in reality, I was bound up in religion. God's love was something I believed had to be earned through striving and good works. So off to work I went. After I graduated from high school, I began studying at an amazing school of Ministry in Redding, California. Even there at this wonderful school filled with thousands of passionate followers of Jesus, the pressure to be a great man of God increased until it became a burden I could no longer bear. It seemed like everywhere I went, students and pastors would come up to me waiting for me to tell them how I led an entire school to Jesus, found the cure for cancer, and ran into a burning house to save an old lady. I couldn't keep up. I couldn't be the perfect Christian no matter how hard I tried or prayed.

Anxiety got the best of me. I couldn't wear a mask anymore, I was losing the battle quickly. I honestly believed that I had to work to earn God's love and approval. If I wasn't living exactly like Jesus and his twelve disciples, I was failing God.

During my second year in ministry school, I cracked and fell into a nervous breakdown. Some would call it "ministry burn out." I was spent. Done. Finished. My old life before I met Jesus seemed easier than this! All I was focused on was what I needed to do for Jesus. What I didn't have a clue about was what Jesus had already done for me. He had loved me all the way all this time, and this truth was what I desperately needed to hear and believe. In the first few years of my walk with Jesus, all I heard through sermons and books were messages about moralism, good works, and methods for ministry. A messiah complex was quickly forming in me, and it was crushing me. I needed grace. I needed love. I needed to know the *real* Jesus.

One day, in the midst of my "burnout," I was lying in bed reading the book of Galatians in the Bible and came across an interesting warning: *"I am shocked that you are turning away so soon from God, who called you to Himself through the loving mercy of Christ. You are following a different way that pretends to be the Good News but is not the Good News at all. You are being fooled by those who deliberately twist the truth concerning Christ. Let God's curse fall on anyone, including us or even an angel in heaven, who preaches a different kind of Good News than the one we preached to you."* What?! I'll be cursed if I don't preach the "Good News?" What even is the Good News?! I came to a realization based on the way I was living that there was no way I knew what the Good News was. If I really knew the Good News, I wouldn't be experiencing so much shame, guilt, and condemnation for all the things I was doing and wasn't doing. I wouldn't be as tired and worn out as I was. If I knew whatever this Good News was, I would be enjoying life! The search for the Good News began, and I wasn't going to preach or serve at church until I discovered what it was.

One day during the year of my search for the Good News, a friend of mine named Eric Fisk noticed my struggle and encouraged me to read *Destined to Reign* by Joseph Prince. So after school, I drove alone to Barnes & Noble to find the book. To be honest, when I found the book in the Christian section, I questioned if it would really have any impact on my life. It looked like a self help book, but I was broken, and I did need some help. I sat there in the bookstore and skimmed through the chapters. One of them caught my eye. The title was "Condemnation Kills," and that rang true for me. Condemnation had been killing me, and I needed to find life from the Savior. I thought God was so mad at me, but through books like this and the kindness of others, I was about to discover that He was actually madly in love with me. As I opened the chapter in the middle of the bookstore, I was utterly shocked at what I read. My heart that was torn by religion was suddenly being mended by the grace of God. My eyes were flooded with tears as I continued reading. I thought to myself: "This is it. This is what I've been missing, this is the Good News."

No more formulas, methods, and striving to earn God's love.

Just Jesus.

Jesus is the Good News, and He changes everything

He will turn every minus into a plus.

He will take any sinner and transform them into a saint.

He will take death and recycle it into life.

During that year, I fell more in love with Jesus than I ever thought I could, because I knew that I was already completely loved by him in the first place. No longer did I need to work *for* God's love, I get to work *from* God's love. As the unconditional love of Jesus saturated my soul once again, the year's pain and the chains of religion fell off and shattered to pieces. My passion for Jesus and love for life was back and better than ever. Life for me became more about knowing the person named Jesus than the principles and traditions of men that have been preached about him. My life has never been the same. I can truthfully say that I am free, happy, and I enjoy living every day as a follower of Jesus. The Good News got me.

As you continue to read my book, you will go on a journey of discovering the Good News of Jesus. I pray that you truly get to know the good and gracious God of the Bible revealed in Jesus Christ. Religion has painted many pictures of God, but only Jesus shows us the true picture of how great God really is. He is the one who pursues the lost, the last, the least, the little, and the lifeless. No matter where you're at in life right now, I believe this book is for you, and in it, you will find grace to live the life God has always intended you to live. I pray that God touches you in a powerful way as you dive into the stories I've written of God's grace and love for us. I truly believe that you will see Jesus and yourself in a new and brighter light as you go on this journey. Let's let go of the good advice and exchange it for the Good News. Let's allow Jesus to take every minus, every loss, and turn them into overwhelming victories.

So faith comes from hearing, that is, hearing the *Good News* about Christ.

Romans 10:17

Chapter One

THE

LOST

"For the Son of Man came to seek and save those who are lost." (Luke 19:10)

I'm one of the few people left in the world who still enjoys some good old Major League Baseball. I have to admit, I almost abandoned it during the steroid and human growth hormone scandals a few years ago, but I've stuck with it. My perseverance paid off in 2016 while watching undoubtedly the greatest World Series in Baseball history. Chicago knows heartbreak, and not just years of it, but generations. Their beloved Cubs hadn't won a World Series in 108 years! No other team in any sport has had a championship drought for as long as the Chicago Cubs. They practically invented the internet meme "Take the L." People would come to games hoisting flags with a big L painted on to it because fans were so used to losing games and playoff series it had almost become comical. They were the biggest losers of baseball. But in the 2016 World Series, the Cubbies ended their century long drought in dramatic fashion. Losers can't lose forever. With the series tied 3-3 to the Cleveland Indians, game seven would be their last shot a becoming world champs. Steven Spielberg couldn't have scripted the scene better than what took place. The tied game went late into the night and was forced to go into extra innings. A 17-minute delay followed the ninth inning, then Cubs hitter Ben Zobrists smacked a tie-breaking RBI double in a two-run

10th that lifted the Cubs to an 8-7 victory over the Indians. "It was like a heavyweight fight, man," said Zobrist, who was named World Series MVP. "Just blow for blow, everybody playing their heart out. The Indians never gave up either, and I can't believe we're finally standing, after 108 years, finally able to hoist the trophy." Game seven of a series in any sport is significant, but this was more than a baseball game to Cubs fans. This win ended more than a century of frustration as the Cubs won their first championship since 1908, ending the longest drought in professional sports. Instead of hoisting the 'L' flags, the wild and relieved fans waved freshly painted 'W' flags all over the stadium and celebrated the city's win into the early morning.

We all love to see losers finally get their win. We have a soft spot for the underdog. And some of us want to see winners get their loss, like the New England Patriots… (cough, cough, I'm from the great Pacific Northwest AKA Seahawks Country). Jesus loves to bring victory to the losers. In his Gospel, the losers always turn out to be the greatest winners.

The social status of the people that Jesus often spent his time with was highly offensive for the prominent, protected, and prolific leaders of his time.

Without a doubt the Pharisees, who were the religious leaders and priests of Israel at the time, had the biggest problem with the friends of Jesus. Like the Cubs, these people were known as the losers, the lost causes, the least likely to do anything significantly great, the lifeless, the little, the last pick in the line. Throughout this book, we are going to look at the 'L's' or labels that the religious leaders would tag people to, and we will discover that they were actually the very people that Jesus loved to spend his time with most. He didn't only love to spend time with these people, he loved to transform their lives. As we look at the 'L's' we will begin to realize that we are currently in the same state as these friends of Jesus, or we have been in this state in our past. We need to be real, not religious. He didn't come for the religious, he came for real hearts, real people, with real issues: *"Healthy people don't need a doctor—sick people do. I have come to call not those who think they are righteous, but those who know they are sinners."* - Jesus. (Mark 2:17)

So here they are, or.. here we are.. let's begin with *the lost*.

Lost means loved.

We are going to unpack three well known stories that Jesus told about three lost things… a sheep, a coin, and a son. Maybe you've heard these stories at church, read them yourself, or are familiar with the famous parable of the prodigal son. I'm going to take a different view on these stories than you may have heard before. But before I do that, we are going to step into the scene and look at who Jesus is telling this story to.

Side note, when we read the Bible, we need to make sure we know the context in which the content is being communicated. Some passages in the Bible are used wildly out of context and have caused hurt and confusion to those that hear it from preachers and teachers who don't take time to properly research the context of the scripture they are using to make their points.

So with at being said, let's look at who Jesus is talking to here: *"Tax collectors and other notorious sinners often came to listen to Jesus teach. This made the Pharisees and teachers of religious law complain that he was associating with such sinful people—even eating with them!" (Luke 15:1-2).*

Jesus is the life of the party.

All throughout the gospels you see Jesus going from dinner party to dinner party. He wasn't meeting in synagogues all day, he was always going to the parties he was invited to. And at this particular dinner party, we have two types of people, people who know they are bad and people who think they are very good. Jesus is about to communicate to everyone at this party the type of people he came to save. Something, or someone, can't be found until it knows it's lost. If we think we are found we don't need a savior.

Jesus says that whoever tries to keep his life or save it will end up losing it, and whoever loses his life for Jesus sake will find it. Jesus came for people who are willing to be losers in order to become a winner. His kingdom is an upside down kingdom. The wise, the worthy, the wonderful, and the winners in their own minds end up being the biggest losers. The least, the lost, the little, the last, and the lifeless end up being the greatest leaders in the kingdom of God. At this particular dinner party with the 'sinners' and so called self pronounced 'saints,' Jesus is about to reveal the heart of each individual at the table with three parables.

Parables are short stories that relate to real life with a moral teaching at the end. They are sort of like riddles with a big mic drop at the end once people find out the hidden meaning. The first parable he tells is about a shepherd with one hundred sheep. As he's walking along the hills of Galilee he realizes that one of his sheep has gone astray. He has one lost sheep, and ninety-nine found sheep. A smart shepherd would take the loss and still be thankful that he's going home with ninety-nine sheep. But this shepherd is not like that. He doesn't want to lose anyone. "No lamb left behind!"

So, what he's about to do is absolutely crazy. He decides to leave ninety-nine sheep behind to go and find the one sheep that lost its way. Are you catching this?! This crazy Shepherd now has one hundred lost sheep! Eventually his scavenger hunt comes to an end and he finds his one lost sheep. Then he does something even more wild, he throws a giant block party for the one sheep that he found. He wasn't angry at the sheep, he didn't reprimand or rebuke the sheep for going astray, he celebrated the fact that he found it.

If you know anything about sheep, you know that they are straight up dumb. Sheep need a shepherd. They have no sense of direction, they are afraid of just about anything and constantly need to be taken care of. This sheep had nothing to do with finding itself. It was completely helpless and lost on its own. If the shepherd decided to never look for this sheep it would've been lost forever. The poor little guy would've never made it back home. So the shepherd isn't celebrating the sheep's good efforts to find its way home or find its way back to the shepherd, the shepherd is celebrating the good news that *he* found the sheep, not the other way around. Jesus finds us, before we ever look for him.

So what is Jesus communicating through this first parable? The one lost sheep represents the sinners at the table. Jesus loves to sit with the lost, because they know they are lost and need to be found by the good shepherd. The ninety-nine sheep that the shepherd let go of to find the one represent the prideful scribes and pharisees.

They all think they're found but sooner or later they are going to realize that they are all just as lost as the lost 'sinners' sitting next to them at the table. We are all sheep, and without the shepherd we are all lost. If we arrogantly think we are found by our own goodness and merit, we are more lost than we could possibly imagine. In order to be found by Jesus, we have to lose our pride and entitlement, and let him find us right where we are at. If you are a Christian reading this right now, think about the way you tell your salvation story (testimony). Most of us usually say that we recited the 'sinner's prayer' or we showed up at a church service and found Jesus. We need to reframe our thinking here.

We didn't run after Jesus to be found, Jesus ran after us! He is the shepherd that ran after the one, and all of us are worth chasing after. You showed up at church or prayed a prayer because God put the desire in you to do it.

You were found in his heart before you were ever lost in your own.

Lost means loved.

Let's lose our pride, and let the shepherd find us right where we are at.

The second parable is about a woman who loses just one out of her ten coins. Her pursuit of one small lost coin is an uncommon one.

This woman spent hours and hours looking for one lost coin while she still had nine in her possession. The typical person would count the loss and move on, but not this woman. She searched throughout her entire house and wouldn't stop until she found her lost coin. These days there are only three things that we would search everywhere for: our cell phones, our wallets, and our keys. I have a confession, I may or may not have driven 20 miles just to go back home after realizing that I left my cell phone there. I hope I'm not the only one guilty of this. We all know that feeling when you do the pocket check. You know, you do a double pat on each pocket.. keys - check.. wallet- check.. phone- check. It's always a funny thing to watch someone have a nervous sweat when they've misplaced their cell phone. For many of us, it's become part of us. We can't leave home without it, and if we do, we will likely turn around and pick it up.

So like us, this woman wouldn't leave her house until she found that coin. Here's the thing about lost materials, they can't move. They don't have a mind of their own and they aren't going to find their owner. The owner has to do 100% of the finding. This is what Jesus is communicating in the second parable: We have no part to play in finding ourselves.

We are like lost coins. The owner has to do all of the finding. Coins don't even call out to the owner. I would like to say that Jesus pursues us whether we call on his name or not. He isn't only after people who are hungry for him. Jesus is looking for the entire world. God is not willing that any would be lost, his mission through Jesus is that all will hopefully be found in him. If one is unaccounted for, Jesus will get out of his seat and run after the one until that one is found. Many of us think that salvation is a 50-50 process or a two-way street, but instead, Jesus alone is salvation and salvation can only be found in and through him. We must decide to trust Jesus for our own lives. For anyone else you know that may seem lost, Jesus sees them and wants them to be found in him more than we know.

Jesus is like the woman who won't leave the house until the one lost coin is found. He is not the kind of person who counts the loss and moves on. He will pursue us all until our last dying breath. He never gives up, he never walks away, his mind is made up about us, he wants us and he will look for us no matter how many times we wind up lost in this journey of life.

Here's what Jesus is trying to tell the Pharisees in the story. The sinners at the table don't know any better. They don't know how to be found. They don't know how to change because they don't know Jesus. Only Jesus Christ brings true transformation. The Savior had to come to the unsaved and offer them a new and better life. Before Jesus, all we know is the world around us, but once we get to know Jesus we see a new and beautiful life, and this new life has no comparison to the old one. Once we experience the abundant life that Jesus offers we will never want to go back to the old one that the enemy (the devil) had us bound to.

Ever since Jesus found me, I've experienced more joy, more peace, more love, and greater friendships than I could have ever imagined. I'm so grateful that I was once a lost coin until he found me!

The last parable that Jesus tells to make his point at the table is my favorite. It's the parable of the prodigal son. We can also call it the parable of the extravagant Father.

So here's how the story goes. There's a father and two sons. One son is a hard-working, valedictorian, varsity letter type of guy. The other is quite different. The younger brother decides to ask his father for his share in the family inheritance before the father even passes away. This type of thing is unheard of in Jewish culture and I would say the same for our culture today.

The father agrees to give the younger son his share of the inheritance and immediately after the son receives it, he packs his things and moves out of the house to spend the next few months partying and living the wildlife, or you can say he was being straight up stupid! His money runs out quickly and he needs to find a job, so he begins working at a farm, cleaning up pig slop. Jesus goes on to say that the younger brother was so hungry that he even wanted to eat the pig food that he was feeding the pigs all day. At this point in the story the Pharisees at the table must have been dropping their jaws in shock and disgust at the younger son. At this time in history, God-fearing Jews and pigs don't get along too well. In the Torah, pigs were considered unclean. For the son to be working around them and wanting to eat their food was absolute rock bottom.

The younger son has quickly become a disgraced, unclean 'sinner.' He comes to a breaking point. This poor and broken son begins to wonder what things are like back home. He remembers that even the servants of his father had a better quality of life then he had. In his mind he thought maybe if he came home, his father would accept him as a servant, but obviously not a son again after all he had done to make a disgrace of the family name and legacy. As the son begins his journey back home, he starts reciting a repentance speech that he would tell his father when they met again. He was going to tell his father that he was sorry for all that he did and if by chance his father forgave him, he would then ask if he could become a servant in his father's house.

In Jewish culture, this was a far stretch considering all that the younger son had done. In their time, if a son had been that disobedient he would've been stoned to death by the father, his family, and the rest of the neighborhood. And that is actually how the original parable ended. Jesus was retelling a well-known parable in Jewish culture and the moral of the story was that if you disobey your parents you should expect a harsh punishment and even possibly death. They took "honor thy father and mother" very seriously. But Jesus has his own version and it doesn't end with death, it ends with new life for this lost son. As the lost son was still a far way off, somehow the father sees him in the distance as if he had been waiting daily for his son's return.

The father gets up out of his seat, leaps off of the front porch, and starts sprinting towards his once lost son. Maybe at this point the son is wondering if there are rocks in the fathers hands as the father is hurrying to get to the son. Does the father have a heart of rage or redemption? The bystanders are also wondering something, where did the father's dignity go!? The man of the house always wore a long robe, so in order for the father to be running to the son he had to have pulled up his robe leaving his old skinny legs bear for everyone to see. Back then, this was a no-no.

It would've been considered public indecency. But the father didn't care about his reputation. He cared about redemption. The father was filled with love and compassion and as he made eye contact with his beloved son. He picked him up, embraced him, and kissed him.

The son was only able to get halfway through his rehearsed repentance speech when the father interrupted him and told his servants to begin serving this once sinful son. Dad loved him far too much. He was home. The father then commands the servants to deck the son out in the father's best robe and sandals, and the family ring on his finger signifying his redemption as a man of the house. But wait, there's more! Just like the first two parables, the father throws an extravagantly wild welcome home party for the son, where the whole town is invited to feast on the family's fattened calf as they celebrate the son's return.

During the party, we witness a new wanderer, the older son. He leaves the party and pouts outside in offense toward his younger brother.

"How did he get off so easy?"

"I work so hard for dad and I never get this star treatment!"

"My brother should've been the one that was killed, not the fattened calf!"

"What kind of father forgives his children that easily?"

"Aren't there conditions to his love?"

"That's cheap, sloppy grace."

"Does my father realize how bad his reputation has become because of my brother?"

The father notices that his older son is missing from the party so he runs outside to find him and embrace him, just as he did earlier that day with the younger son. Two lost sons. One lost in sin, one in religion. Both were equally lost. Every pharisee as the table could relate to the older brother, and so can I. We can get lost in religion as easily as much as we can get lost in sin, and the good news is that our heavenly father pursues us all no matter how lost we become or how we became lost in the first place. Jesus loves the Pharisees just as much as He loves the sinners at the table, and He reveals this so well through this last parable. The older brother was embraced by grace as the father explained to him that he already owned everything the father owned. He could have thrown the same party any day.

Here's what the Pharisees needed to understand:
they should've realized that they already were children of God, and the mission of Jesus was to seek after lost sons and daughters and bring them back home to His Father. Religion can blind us from the amazing grace of God. When a broken soul returns to Jesus, let's celebrate them, not condemn them. Jesus is a better picture of the older brother

in this story, instead of sulking outside, he pursues the lost, alongside his dad, and persuades the world that we have a Father of kindness and mercy, a Father who is willing to embrace the worst of the worst. Jesus reveals on the cross, with His arms stretched wide, the same posture of God the Father, who proclaims that we are worth it, not worthless. Our worth isn't revealed in our works, it's revealed in the eyes of Jesus as he embraced the cross. Just as the Father embraced his sons, Jesus gladly embraced the cross, knowing that through his suffering, salvation would come to millions upon millions of lost sons and daughters. Our Savior was willing to lose his reputation with the religious for the sake of sinners. He is wild with his grace.

Whether you find yourself lost in sin or lost in religion right now, we are all worth pursuing. Let the Father run to you. Let Him find you. Let him embrace you, kiss you, and throw his robe of grace upon you.

Here's the good news, we have a Father that runs to us, not from us.

Lost means loved.

And the *Good News* about the Kingdom will be preached throughout the whole world, so that all nations will hear it.

Matthew 24:14

Chapter Two

THE

LEAST

"Don't lie to each other, for you have stripped off your old nature and all its wicked deeds. Put on your new nature and be renewed as you learn to know your Creator and become like Him." (Colossians 3:9-10).

One day as I was browsing through the book of Mark, I stumbled upon a familiar story that soon became much more meaningful than what is seen at face value. At first glance, we see Jesus performing a miracle for a blind beggar, but let me take you a little deeper. The story goes like this: Jesus is leaving town, and on the outskirts of it, the poor and the blind camp out waiting for tourists to give them some spare change. One of the men, "blind Bartimaeus," hears that Jesus is passing by and shouts at the top of his lungs for Jesus' attention. Let me stop here and tell you that the blind and the poor were designated a spot to beg, far away from the middle and upper class scene. I'm not quite sure how long Bart was begging, but the poor man had no other choice. He would be the least likely person for Christ, a man with great stature, to approach... right? It was Jewish law for him to stay in the begging quarters of town. The crowd shuns Bart as he calls out to the king of kings, but he shouts to Jesus even louder the second time. Bartimaeus has the floor; Jesus is all ears, *"'Tell him to come here.' So they called the blind man. 'Cheer up', they said. 'Come on, He's calling you!' Bartimaeus threw aside his coat, jumped up, and came to Jesus. 'What do you want me to do for you?' Jesus asked. 'My Rabbi,' the blind man said, 'I want to see!'*

And Jesus said to him, 'Go, for your faith has healed you.' Instantly the man could see, and he followed Jesus down the road." (Mark 10:49-52).

When we read the Bible, it's important to realize that every single sentence has a purpose. God inspired every word in the book, so as I read this story, I stopped and wondered why the author mentioned the detail of Bartimaeus throwing off his cloak. So I did some research. What I learned was that not only did beggars have to stay in a corner of town, they also had to wear cloaks/coats that were designed to show others that they were blind and homeless. He was an untouchable. An outcast. While he couldn't see himself, everyone else had put an identity on him with their own eyes.

Most days, our clothing communicates and even defines who we are. When I say the word hipster, I'm guessing you're imagining an hombre hat, perfectly trimmed beards, faux prescription glasses, red and black flannel shirts, leather, skinny jeans, a good cup of coffee and did I say leather? What about Hypebeast? Supreme. More Supreme. Off-White, and countless palm to face selfies. When I worked at Nordstrom, I was required to wear a slim fit suit, shirt, and tie, with freshly shined shoes every day. When people ran into me outside of work, they would often guess my occupation correctly or that I was a lawyer. Nordstrom headquarters wants people to know who they are as a company based on what their employees dress like on the job. They want their people to dress the best because they strive to sell the highest quality brands, and not to mention amazing customer service.

Like myself, Bartimaeus was required to dress a certain way every day, except his outfit was not going to be found in any GQ article. He was looking more like Derrick Zoolander in the 'Derelicte' campaign. Bartimaeus was defined by his clothing. When he wore the coat, everyone knew he was a helpless blind beggar. But before Jesus even healed the man of his blindness, Bart threw off his coat as he marched to Jesus. He knew that God was about to give him a brand new identity, and he would never be known as the 'blind beggar' again.

Many of us subconsciously define ourselves by the things we do, or don't do. As a result, we put on a coat so to speak, of shame, guilt, and condemnation. We think we are the least likely people for Jesus to accept, love, and take in. But the truth is, we are the exact people that Jesus desires to sit with at his table. I've met some people that have been defining themselves by one mistake they made over 10 years ago. Whether it's failures or successes, our society is quick to give themselves titles based on their latest action.

You might be reading this right now, knowing that the touchdown pass you threw on Friday night under the lights defines you. Or maybe it was the website you got caught looking at. I'm here to tell you something amazing, Jesus never defines us by what we do or don't do. He defines us by what *he did* for us on the cross over 2,000 years ago. When Jesus died on the cross for us, our sins, mistakes, and failures died with him. The good news is, three days later when Jesus rose from the grave, our sins still remained in the tomb, dead and gone. All of us were once called sinners because of the original sin of Adam and Eve, but Jesus came to give us a new identity:

"Yes, Adam's one sin brings condemnation for everyone, but Christ's one act of righteousness brings a right relationship with God and new life for everyone. Because one person disobeyed God, many became sinners. But because one other person obeyed God, many will be made righteous." (Romans 5:18-19).

As you can see in this passage, we were once defined by our sins and failures. "If you sin, you are a sinner." But now that Jesus has come, we're no longer defined by our sins and mistakes, we're defined by him and him alone! And what does he say we are? Righteous! This good news is hard to swallow for many. Too many Christians accept Jesus but forget to accept all that Jesus has done for them. Righteous people are wearing shabby jackets with false labels on them, and it's time to take them off and leave them on the hanger for good.

You are not your mistakes. You are His masterpiece.

Your identity is not found in what you do, it is found in what Jesus did.

God isn't mad at us, He's madly in love with us.

Now, let's help others take off the same coats we once wore, so that they can run the race with Jesus.

Reach The Least

There is no greater miracle to witness than seeing someone find salvation in Jesus. Ever since I gave my life to Jesus in high school, I have been burning to see the world come to the same salvation that met me. God instantly put a fire in my heart to see people come to Christ. From the moment I turned to God, I have been bringing others with me into His family. Through preaching and street evangelism, I have had the honor of leading over 3,000 people to Jesus and baptising over 200 in the last 8 years of following Him.

Have you ever lead someone to Christ before? If you are a Christian, it is our calling. This isn't just for pastors, missionaries and evangelists. If you have been given the great gift of eternal life, your purpose now is to freely give it to everyone in your circle. The Bible says, *"The fruit of the righteous is a tree of life, And he who is wise wins souls."* *(Proverbs 11:30).* If you need some inspiration and fire in your bones, here are some stories from my life that keep me going and keep me grounded in the main thing, soul winning. Winning and loving the very least.

It was a beautiful, blue skied fourth of July in Gig Harbor, Washington. My brother Jonah and I decided to spend the afternoon helping my uncle Greg sell kettle corn and lemonade. Suddenly there was a lull in business and instead of taking a lunch break, Jonah and I went to go walk the beach. As we walked along, I had an idea, "Jonah, let's find the biggest, most scary looking crowd and preach the good news of Jesus to them!" He agreed, so the search began.

Immediately under a bridge, we noticed a crowd of about 30 teenagers crowded around, smoking marijuana, drinking, and breaking things… rock n' roll. I suggested we keep walking as fear enveloped me and beads of nervous sweat began to drip down my forehead. But Jonah insisted, "Dude, we aren't going to find a better crowd than this, it was your idea, let's go!"

As we approached the group, my heart was pounding with anxiety, and all of the sudden words came out of my mouth but I wasn't even thinking! I said, "Excuse me everyone! I have an announcement to make!" A few people yelled at me and said "We don't want to hear about Jesus!" I was surprised they knew I was a Christian.. I hadn't mentioned Jesus yet and I wasn't dressed with the common white button up shirt, tie, and name tag inscribed "Elder Jacob." I went on and told the crowd my own story of how Jesus changed me in an instant, and how His love is better than all of the experiences and substances I had ever tried. I asked them if anyone would like to follow Jesus and receive some prayer from my brother and I. A young man named Chris came right up to us as the rest of the crowd dispersed. He told me that He wanted to be a Jesus' follower and he also wanted to be filled with the Holy Spirit. And just like that, we prayed for Chris and he was instantly filled with the Spirit of God. What seemed to be the leader of the pack came up to us and asked us what we were doing to Chris. Before I could get a word out Chris replied, "Jesus filled me with His love and Spirit. I feel so good, you need this man!" He walked away saying, "I wish you could fill me with satan instead." Chris wasn't moved by this. By the assurance in his eyes, I could see I was looking at a new man. He left Jonah and I that day filled with courage to reach his friends and offer the same free gift of salvation that he had received that day.

The Good News of Jesus is irresistible when it is presented right. In fact, I have seen people give their lives to Jesus in a matter of minutes after meeting them. On one occasion, my friend and I went to the grocery store for a late night snack, and there was a young employee standing in an isle stocking shelves. I approached him and asked if I can read him a scripture that had stuck out to me that day: "Beloved, I pray that all may go well with you and that you may be in good health, as it goes well with your soul" (3 John 2). After reading the verse to him, I asked if his soul was well. He said it wasn't, so I asked him if he wanted his soul to be well and he said yes! Right there in the isle, we prayed together and he gave his life to Jesus, the only God able to give us a happy and healthy soul. My friend Arnaud and I walked away shocked that we lead a man to Jesus in just two minutes. We honestly couldn't stop laughing all the way back home. Can leading people to Jesus really be this easy? The answer is yes! People are starving for hope, and when they are given a solution for their empty and burdened souls, they will come running to that answer.

After I began seeing people come to Jesus at such a rapid rate like this, I just couldn't help myself! I started preaching in public and inviting people to follow Jesus everywhere I went. A group of my friends and I went to go see one of the Chronicles of Narnia movies in theaters, and halfway through the movie, I decided that I was going to preach at the end during the credits. Once I made that decision, my heart doubled in beats per minute for the rest of the movie. I had no idea what I was going to say, but all I knew was that God wanted me to say something, and I trusted that when I opened my mouth, God would fill it with His words.

Once the movie ended and the credits began to roll, I walked to the front of the theater and shouted, "Excuse me everyone, my name is Jacob and I want you all to know that the kingdom that Aslan talked about is very similar to the one Jesus talked about in the Bible, and if you want to enter into that kingdom all you need to do is accept King Jesus and follow him for the rest of your life. I'll be down here ready to pray for anyone who would like to make that decision, thank you!" Many of the moviegoers left, but some stayed behind to receive prayer, and one person waited for the rest of the crowd to leave. Once the room was empty, this man got up from his seat and ran to me and my friends with tears falling from his face. He hugged me and asked if he could give his life to Jesus! Right there in the theater, as the credits rolled, a young man was being transformed by the love of Jesus. He even began to start attending our church on Sundays.

Lastly, my friend Arnaud and I were out in downtown Redding, California, praying for the homeless. A man walked out of a local restaurant and noticed that we were praying for people. He urgently walked up to us with tears in his eyes saying, "I saw you both praying, please pray for me right now if you can, I have lung cancer and have only few months left to live. I don't want to leave my wife and family yet. Do you believe Jesus can heal me?"

We both shouted, "YES!" Arnaud and I prayed, and this man felt the power of God touch his body from his head to his feet. He exclaimed, "The pain is all gone! The fatigue is gone! I feel brand new!" That man never died of cancer, he still is alive and well today. People are drawn to Jesus. He is the desire of the world, whether they know it or not. No matter how great or urgent the need, Jesus is able to meet it.

You can do this too. I don't have 'secret to soul winning success'. I just started telling people about Jesus and how he changed my life. All you need to do is open your mouth, and God will fill it with His word. Open your hands and God will fill them with healing for the broken. Open your heart to Him and He will fill it with love and compassion for the lost, and the very least.

But you must continue to believe this truth and stand firmly in it. Don't drift away from the assurance you received when you heard the *Good News*. The *Good News* has been preached all over the world, and I, Paul, have been appointed as God's servant to proclaim it.

Colossians 1:23

Chapter Three

THE LIFE- LESS

"Jesus Christ did not come to make bad people good, but to make dead people alive." - Ravi Zacharias

This topic will be digested easiest with a parable, one about a Pharisee and a Publican. One "good" man, and one notoriously bad man.

This comes from Luke, chapter 18, verses 9-14: *"Jesus also told this parable to some who trusted themselves that they were righteous and despised everybody else. Two men went up to the temple to pray: one, a Pharisee, the other, a tax collector. The Pharisee stood apart by himself and prayed thus: 'God, I thank you that I am not like the others are, greedy, unjust, adulterers – and I thank you especially that I am not like this tax collector. I fast two days every week and I give you a tenth of all my income.' But the tax collector stood a long way off and would not even raise his eyes to heaven. Instead, he beat on his breast and said, 'O God, be merciful to me, a sinner.' I tell you this man went to his house justified rather than the other: for everyone who exalts himself will be humbled, but he who humbles himself will be exalted."*

Amen.

Now, the first thing that I need to mention is the fact that this parable is not just a simple lesson on the virtue of humility. There's much more to it than that. It is a message on the futility of religion – it's a comedic one based on the idea that there is anything at all you can do to get yourself right with God. It is about the madness if even trying. Therefore, it is not a simple recommendation to obtain a humble religious stance instead of a proud one; it's a warning to let go of all religious, moral and ethical stances when you're trying to take hold of your own justification before God. This is, in short, a message and call to move on to the main point of the Good News: have faith alone in the God who raises the dead.

Let's consider both characters in Jesus' parable. But first, forget about all of the prejudice you may have about Pharisees. Give this Pharisee all the moral credit that you can. After all, he is a good man. By our world's standards he is a very good man.

He's not a criminal, not a lazy man, not a womanizer. He doesn't take anything that he hasn't earned, he's a generous giver, he's faithful to his wife, patient with his kids, and consistent with his friends. He's nothing like the tax collector, who is the worst type of thief: a legal one. The tax collector has the rights to be a crook for a living. He's a mafia-like man working with the Roman government, that is allowing him to collect hard earned cash from his fellow Jews. The Romans have a hard time finding them, but of course, he knows their whereabouts and speaks their language. He can take all the money he wants, as long as he pays back the Roman government an agreed set fee. For years, he's been thriving off the work of his hard working Jewish brothers and sisters, wealthy enough to roll out in a in a Bentley Coupe with designer loafers.

But the Pharisee, he's not only a good man; he's a religious one. Not necessarily in a bad way either. His outward upright character is marked with inward discipline. I mean, who else is fasting twice a week and regularly giving ten percent of their income to God? This guy. Any mega church would give an arm and a leg to have a guy like that sign up for their internship. To top it all off, this guy even thanks God for the happy life he has. Now remember, the author Luke tells us that Jesus spoke this story to anyone who trusted in their own righteousness. But, Jesus shows us that this man comes to the temple to give glory to God. There's nothing wrong with that, right?

So, what is Jesus trying to tell us about this good man... about this man who would be a proper candidate to take the role of head pastor at your local church? Jesus tells us that he's in bad shape. But not just bad shape – this Pharisee is in a worse state that a rotten tax collector who just waltzes into the temple with no gift, no righteousness, just a small confession.

I know that we would all accept the Pharisee into our churches and even our homes. But, would you accept the man who has his hand in the offering basket to pay for cars and prostitutes? Would it be enough for that man to come into your church on a Sunday, stare at his shoes and say, "God, I'm a sinner, will you please be merciful to me?" Maybe we are saying we would forgive him and have mercy on him... but, really, would we? I'm not sure. That's up to you to decide, but God says that he sure would according to this parable. Let's look at this moment from God's point of view.

God is sitting on his throne, never sleeping, never taking a break, busy holding all creation in place- thinking and speaking things into existence, patiently placing all the hairs on your head, making sure the rooster crows each morning, causing the earth to revolve around the sun, caring for the homeless and the widow, while at the same time bringing peace and wisdom to generals in the Pentagon. And now, in walk these two men. The Pharisee proudly walks right up to God, pulls up a chair to the King's table and whips out a deck of playing cards. He opens the pack, bridges them, does a couple of slick card tricks, throws in a few one-handed cuts and a shuffle. He then hands the deck over to God, and says, "Go 'head. Cut. I'm right in the middle of a winning streak." But, God looks at the Pharisee with a disappointed smile, gently moves the deck away and tell him, "Maybe not. Maybe your luck just ran out son."

But the Pharisee is persistent. He picks up the deck and begins to deal God a three of fasting and a king of no adultery. God says, "Hey, I don't think you understand, this isn't your game. I really don't want to take all your money here."

"Come on, God," says the Pharisee.

"How about just one game of blackjack, or what about some Texas hold 'em?" I've been real lucky with Texas hold 'em lately!"

At this point, God begins to look a bit annoyed and says, "Look son, I really mean it. Don't play me – the odds will always be on my side. You'd be wise to be like the other guy who came in here with you. He ditched his cards in the trash can on the way here. How about you both just take a drink on the house and head back home?"

Have you caught what Jesus has been saying in this parable?

He is saying that no matter how hard the Pharisee works or how good his life may look, there is no shot at winning the game of justification… he's no better off than the tax collector here. In fact, the Pharisee is worse off; both men are losers, but only the tax collector realizes this and is trusting God's offer of a drink on the house.

Both men are dead.

The only hope in this parable is in the God who can raise the dead!

"But, wait a second…" you may be saying. Can't we give the Pharisee a little bit of credit here for his godliness? Isn't there a little more life in him then the sinful tax collector?

If we believe that, we are making the very same miscalculation as this Pharisee. Dead is dead, death is death. The tax collector has discovered the good news. He's come to an absolute end of himself. He knows that he's finished in this rat race, and only Jesus can deal with him at this point. But, the Pharisee on the other hand, believes that his sack full of good deeds will carry him through for the rest of his life.

The Pharisee may be right, and he will be fine for the rest of his life. But what about the length of eternity with God? What about us? Let's suppose for a moment that we are even better than the Pharisee in this story. Let's assume that we are not tempted to any sin except the sin of envy. And even there, you believe that you will never fall into the trap for the remainder of your life here on earth. But are you sure that you are strong enough to say no to that sin, forever? Maybe the only reason you were able to conquer it is because you were lacking in the opportunity to fall into it. This has happened many times for me personally. Have you ever believed in yourself to be immune to a certain sin or vice only to find later that that you fell into it when the temptation was strong enough? The man who resists the five-dollar offer sometimes gives into a five-million-dollar one. The loyal friend who would never betray his friend may do it if they discovered that their friend was about to betray them. The pastor immune to the corruption of power finds corruption easier as he gains power.

Take your dormant dose of envy to heaven with you then. From now till the last day of your life on earth you may never find the opportunity to fall into that sin. But in eternity – in the place where there are no limits to opportunity, where you will literally have forever to meet anyone and everyone there – is your selflessness so profound that you can positively tell me that you will never find someone you are jealous of? Is the iron armor of your humility that strong and mighty?

There is the problem as God sees it. We have no goodness apart from Jesus (Psalm 16). When we think we can gain a life apart from him, we deceive ourselves, and the empires of sand we build will soon crumble into nothingness. True life, true greatness comes when we give God our dead works. Life comes when he raises us into it. Don't strive for it, sink into it.

What Jesus is saying in this story is that there is absolutely no amount of human goodness or effort that is good enough to pass his test, and therefore, God is not willing to take a risk on us and our human trust in works. He will not take our clutter, and baggage, as we hold onto it, into his Kingdom. But, he will certainly take the clean emptiness of our death and will recycle it in the power of Jesus resurrection. The Pharisee is condemned because he takes a stand on a life God just cannot use. God commends the tax collector because he gives God something he can use... A dead man. The tax collector sees the truth. His efforts are not necessary, because it's all about Christ's efforts on the cross. We lose sight of grace when we live under the reign of bookkeeping. As we keep score of our good works and religion, we lose Jesus in the process. You can only gain Jesus when you let go of yourself. We must let go of our own trust in self redemption. It is miserable to keep count of what God is no longer counting. The Pharisee was counting on himself, the tax collector was counting on grace.

Hopefully by now, you see my point and have concluded that the Pharisee is a fool. You are right. But, if you have also come to conclude that he is a rare breed of a fool, you are wrong. So many of us make the same mistake as the Pharisee day by day. We love grace, but are so quick to run back to works and justification by our own efforts.

Let me prove it to you. Now let's say the tax collector goes home justified, just as he does in Jesus' parable. Imagine his week after this God encounter... What will his life look like? Will it be reformed? Does he quit is terrible job as a scheming tax collector? Does he repay everyone for his wrongs? Does he join a local prayer group or Bible study? What if he does none of that? What if he goes home clean, justified by God, yet doesn't do one single thing during the week to change his ways? Now, a week of the same wicked living has gone by and he goes back up to the temple and prays the same prayer to the Lord. I tell you, he will still come home justified, clean, and forgiven. But you don't like that do you. You're confronted by the unfairness of this. The sinful rat got off free!

We want the tax collector to come back the second time with the Pharisee's speech in his pocket! This is hilarious.

We want him to come to Jesus, boasting about the sudden life change for righteousness, as if this would impress God. What we miss here is that he was already loved by Jesus, regardless of the good or bad. He never confessed that his heart was in the right place, he confessed that he was dead.

And that's where life comes in. Let us never become puffed up by our own works.

All of us long to establish our own identity by becoming approved in everyone's eyes. We spend our days tirelessly striving for acceptance, people pleasing from the moment we wake up to the time we lay down at night. From social media to the workplace, our lives are filled with score cards. Truthfully, we hate this parable from Jesus because it plainly reveals the truth of our condition. We are afraid of the tax collector's acceptance because we know exactly what it means. It means that we will never be free until we we are completely dead to our efforts of justifying ourselves. For most of us, that business of self justifying is our entire life, and that is why we must lay it down. We will never experience the wonderful grace of Jesus until we let it go. Grace needs to be taken straight. If you add works to the equation you no longer have grace.

Jesus came to raise the dead. He didn't come to make bad people good. He didn't come to improve the improvable. He came to make dead people live. As long as we live like the Pharisee, alive in our own eyes, we will continue to resent the scandal of Jesus, the scandal of his grace. Once we are able to admit that we are like the tax collector, that we are dead, only then will be be able to stop scoffing at grace.

Let's face it. This admittedly is a terrifying step to take. You will likely scream and cry and flail around before you take it, because it means cutting yourself out of life's great game. For many of us, it's the only game we know. Let me give you some comfort. Here are three things I've discovered in taking this step. First, it's only one step! Second, it's a step out of a lie, a step from fiction to fact. And third, like myself, you will laugh so hard when you discover how easy it all really was, and how short the trip is to Jesus and his grace. You were already there.

When we come to Jesus, we must realize that only true life can come through him. Before I knew him I was dead on the inside and because of that my life produced death. I destroyed so many things all around me, simply because his real and everlasting life wasn't yet flowing through my veins. I needed a touch of heaven. We all do. Before I met Jesus and let him transform me, I was alive but I wasn't truly living. I had a heartbeat but my heart wasn't truly beating. I still remember the first time I felt God's presence, it felt like breathing for the first time. I felt free, and I knew I belonged. I came alive in his presence, and I've been living with purpose ever since.

Death is the doorway to resurrection - the only way to become born again. Die to yourself, so you can finally live with him.

We are either dead or alive, there is no in between.

Life is a person. There is no true life apart from Jesus.

"I am the resurrection and the life. Anyone who believes in me will live, even after dying." -Jesus (John 11:25).

If you try to hang on to your life, you will lose it. But if you give up your life for my sake and for the sake of the *Good News*, you will save it.

Mark 8:35

Life Through Forgiveness

"To forgive is divine." - Alexander Pope

Only through Jesus can we truly forgive with our hearts.

If we cannot forgive we cannot truly live.

If we're going to talk about forgiveness, we have to jump straight to the book of Matthew, chapter 18. I've grown up reading this passage of scripture in my home, and small groups, and I have taught it many times to my students in my classroom. Many of us use what I'm about to present to you as a textbook for "healthy" confrontation. Or some use it as three strike rule for excommunicating people. Recently, I believe the Lord has given me a revelation that has shown me a deeper meaning into the heart of this passage of scripture.

Here's the context: Jesus is sitting with his disciples explaining to them what his kingdom looks like, what greatness looks like, and how he has a heart to seek all who are lost. Then, the topic of confrontation and forgiveness is brought up: *"If your brother sins against you, go and tell him his fault, between you and him alone. If he listens to you, you have gained your brother. But if he does not listen, take one or two others along with you, that every charge may be established by the evidence of two or three witnesses. If he refuses to listen to them, tell it to the church. And if he refuses to listen even to the church, let him be to you as a Gentile and a tax collector." (Matthew 18:15-17 ESV).*

At first glance it seems to look like a three strike rule. And that is what many of us believe today if you are familiar with Christianity and church culture. We are supposed to confront somebody one on one, and if they don't change, confront them at your small group, and if they still aren't changing, confront them in a large group. If they don't change after that, kick them out! Get them out of here, and tell them that you never want to see them again!

Just kidding.

But I have heard people teach it that way, and I'm sure some of you have as well. Let's go back to the last line of this passage to see how we should treat people who simply won't change: *"If he refuses to listen to them, tell it to the church. And if he refuses to listen even to the church, let him be to you as a Gentile and a tax collector." (Matthew 18:17 ESV).* Jesus never tells us to kick people out, he tells us to treat people like Gentiles and tax collectors. So let's look at the context here. Let me ask you this question, how did Jesus treat Gentiles and tax collectors? Well, the author of this chapter that we're reading right now, Matthew, was a disciple of Jesus and also happened to be a former tax collector. The Pharisees, who were the religious leaders of that time, often accused Jesus of spending too much time with sinners and tax collectors. There is not one time in all four Gospels that recount the life and ministry of Jesus, where you can find Jesus excommunicating a Gentile or tax collector. But you sure can find many times where Jesus is seeking out and loving Gentiles and tax collectors.

Let's read the calling of Matthew-Levi the Tax Collector here: *"He went out again beside the sea, and all the crowd was coming to him, and he was teaching them. And as he passed by, he saw Levi the son of Alphaeus sitting at the tax booth, and he said to him, 'Follow me.' And he rose and followed him. And as he reclined at table in his house, many tax collectors and sinners were reclining with Jesus and his disciples, for there were many who followed him. And the scribes of the Pharisees, when they saw that he was eating with sinners and tax collectors, said to his disciples, 'Why does he eat with tax collectors and sinners?' And when Jesus heard it, he said to them, 'Those who are well have no need of a physician, but those who are sick. I came not to call the righteous, but sinners.'"(Mark 2:13-17 ESV).*

So here is the moral of the story, if your brother is still not changing after multiple failures and confrontation, you are supposed to treat them in the same way that Jesus treated Gentiles and tax collectors. What does that mean? It means giving them even more grace than you would for a fellow Christian. It means don't give up on them. Keep pursuing them. Instead of judging and correcting, try loving and listening. Don't kick them out, bring them in. They may be dead, but you can bring them back to life.

The funny thing about this passage of scripture is that Peter, one of Jesus' disciples, seems to be stumped on the story and still thinks it's about the three strike rule that most of us follow today in our modern world. He thinks that there is a limit to how many times we should forgive. He is worried about it only being "three" times, so he tries to stretch it.. *"Then Peter came up and said to him, 'Lord, how often will my brother sin against me, and I forgive him? As many as seven times?' Jesus said to him, 'I do not say to you seven times, but seventy-seven times.'" (Matthew 18:21-22 ESV).* Peter thought seven was a good and spiritual number, "Well, seven is the number of completion, so it must be the limit to my forgiveness." Jesus answered him back with 70×7, which has two powerful meanings that actually have nothing to do with a math equation. This isn't the first time we see 70×7 in Scripture. We have to see where this phrase was first mentioned to better grasp the meaning of it. So let's jump to the book of Genesis chapter four, the very first book of the Bible.

The first time 70×7 was mentioned, it came out of the mouth of an angry and strong man named Lamech. Here's what he had to say: *"Lamech said to his wives: 'Adah and Zillah, hear my voice; you wives of Lamech, listen to what I say: I have killed a man for wounding me, a young man for striking me. If Cain's revenge is sevenfold, then Lamech's is seventy-sevenfold.'" (Genesis 4:23-24 ESV)*

He is increasing the curse of Cain to anybody who hurts him. This is like the ultimate curse of all curses. This man had some anger issues. For reference, here's the curse that Cain received for killing his brother Abel: *"And the Lord said, 'What have you done? The voice of your brother's blood is crying to me from the ground. And now you are cursed from the ground, which has opened its mouth to receive your brother's blood from your hand. When you work the ground, it shall no longer yield to you its strength. You shall be a fugitive and a wanderer on the earth.' Cain said to the Lord, 'My punishment is greater than I can bear. Behold, you have driven me today away from the ground, and from your face I shall be hidden. I shall be a fugitive and a wanderer on the earth, and whoever finds me will kill me.' Then the Lord said to him, 'Not so! If anyone kills Cain, vengeance shall be taken on him sevenfold.' And the Lord put a mark on Cain, lest any who found him should attack him." (Genesis 4:10-15 ESV).*

Lamech really put some heat on that curse. It would be a good idea to avoid that guy at all costs! So let's jump back to Matthew chapter eighteen, where Jesus mentioned 70×7. Jesus is saying that your forgiveness should be the polar opposite of the anger in Lamech's heart. Lamech had a heart of vengeance, but Jesus had a heart of reconciliation and redemption. Lamech wanted to bind people, but Jesus sought to release people from their burdens and shame. The second meaning of 70×7 is incredible. The Hebrew culture is fascinated with numerology. Nearly every number has a meaning. In fact, I have the numbers 555 tattooed on my wrist, which means perfect and infinite grace. In Hebrew, the number 490, the sum of 70×70, means infinitely perfect - complete. Jesus is asking us to have complete forgiveness, perfect forgiveness, infinite forgiveness, to the people who sin against us and wrong us. This passage of scripture is not about numbers or limits. It's about the heart. He wants our hearts to be full, and complete with infinite forgiveness and love!

If we still don't get it yet, that's OK. Jesus tells us one more story in Matthew chapter 18 to further illustrate his point on having complete and infinite forgiveness. The last teaching he gives us in this chapter is a parable about a king and a servant who owed the king a large sum of money. The servant of the king owed him an unforgivable amount, an amount so high it would be impossible to ever repay. I'll let Jesus tell you the rest of the story: *"And since he could not pay, his master ordered him to be sold, with his wife and children and all that he had, and payment to be made. So the servant fell on his knees, imploring him, 'Have patience with me, and I will pay you everything.' And out of pity for him, the master of that servant released him and forgave him the debt." (Matthew 18:25-27 ESV).*

Amazing, right? What a gracious King! Unfortunately this is not the end of the story, as the King's gracious heart did not rub off on his servant who had been forgiven the impossible debt.

Here's how it all ends: *"But when that same servant went out, he found one of his fellow servants who owed him a hundred denarii, and seizing him, he began to choke him, saying, 'Pay what you owe.' So his fellow servant fell down and pleaded with him, 'Have patience with me, and I will pay you.' He refused and went and put him in prison until he should pay the debt. When his fellow servants saw what had taken place, they were greatly distressed, and they went and reported to their master all that had taken place. Then his master summoned him and said to him, 'You wicked servant! I forgave you all that debt because you pleaded with me. And should not you have had mercy on your fellow servant, as I had mercy on you?' And in anger his master delivered him to the jailers, until he should pay all his debt. So also my heavenly Father will do to every one of you, if you do not forgive your brother from your heart."* (Matthew 18:28-35 ESV).

The servant didn't get it. Like Peter, and like many of us, we think forgiveness is all about numbers and keeping score. That is not the way of Jesus. In this parable, Jesus happens to be the king. The servant did not understand the incredible decision that the king had made. In forgiving the servant, the king was ultimately deciding to lay down a life of bookkeeping, and remembering the faults of our past. True love keeps no record of wrongs as the apostle Paul states, and that is exactly what this king, or Jesus, is doing. Jesus did not come to keep score, he came to settle the score when he died on the cross, ultimately laying down the gavel of judgment once and for all. We will end up like this servant if we choose to live a life of keeping score. That way of living is hell on earth.

Our job is not to judge others, it's to love them unconditionally. Just as Jesus has completely and infinitely loved us and forgiven us all. By choosing a life of unforgiveness, we are throwing ourselves in a prison of hurt and torment. When we don't forgive, we hurt ourselves more than the person we choose not to forgive. No matter how many times someone has wronged you, Jesus' command remains the same: Love your neighbor as yourself. Forgive them. This may seem like an impossible task, and let me tell you the truth, it will be if you don't have Jesus living inside of your heart. Unforgiveness is like a cancer, and I don't want anyone reading this book to go on living this way. So let's stop, take a deep breath, and talk to Jesus. We've all been hurt before, and I'm sure all of us have hurt others. Before we move on I think there's something that we need to do. Let's invite Jesus in to help us both forgive and ask others for forgiveness.

Pray with me: Dear Jesus, please come right now and fill my heart with your love. There is no way I can do this without you. Only you have enough infinite love to forgive me for all the things I've done to you, and to help me forgive the people who have wronged me. I need you to please help me lay down a life of bookkeeping just like you laid your life down on the cross and forgave the people who persecuted you and nailed you to that tree. Today I'm asking you to help me forgive (fill in the blank), for the times they (fill in the blank). I don't want to hold this against them anymore, and I want to love them just like you still love me. Please heal me from the wounds that have hurt my heart and from the times I've been wronged. I don't want to do this to others, so please give me courage to ask others that I've hurt in the past to forgive me for how I've wronged them. All my life I've lived like the world, keeping score. But today I'm choosing to live a different way. I'm choosing to live like you; forgiving and loving unconditionally. Thank you for being here with me. Without you I could never do what I just did! Praise God!

Keep praying like this, it's not a one time thing! But if you prayed this prayer, you are moving in the right direction! You are walking in the footsteps of Jesus, with Jesus!

Let's live to forgive every day.

For I am not ashamed of this *Good News* about Christ. It is the power of God at work,

saving everyone who believes—the Jew first and also the Gentile.

Romans 1:16

Life In The Midst of Death

It was 9pm on a hot night in the middle of August. My wife, Mariah, turned the A/C on full blast and hopped into bed with me. Little did I know that I was minutes from receiving a phone call from my mom that would lead to one of most difficult and grievous 24 hours of my life. The phone vibrated from under my pillow, and as I swiped my touch screen to answer, all I could hear was my mom sobbing and screaming, "Jacob drive to your grandma's house, you need to bring her to the hospital, Greg is hurt."

Those were the only words she could get out at the time.

My Uncle Greg (my mom's brother), had been battling Parkinson's disease for over 5 years and 2015 was the worst of them all. At the beginning of the year, things started spiraling downhill quickly with side effects from the medication he was taking, and the overall toll the disease had taken on his body and mind. When I heard that he was hurt, I just figured he had crashed his car, or slipped and fell and my mom was only worked up because of her love for her brother. Writing this now, I wish it was just a fall or a car accident, but my friend Anson called on my way to my grandma's and told me it was much worse. Greg shot himself in the head and was on life support. My blood thickened and my muscles tensed up all at once. All I could say as I drove the car was, "NO! Jesus, NO!"

I helped my grandma get to the car and as we all arrived at the hospital, I knew that this would be the last few moments that I would get to see my uncle Greg here on earth. Up until this moment, I had never cried so hard and felt so angry and defeated all at the same time. When you cry that hard you feel like all the air is being squeezed out of you. You feel like time stops. All you want to do is run away but you know that not even that could help cure the pain.

Greg helped me find grace. He helped me discover this Good News. Greg was a light to hundreds. He loved me so well, and constantly called out the gold in my life. His vibrant life still inspires me and many others today.

The news spread about what had happened. My phone started blowing up with calls and texts. I began to wonder, "Is this really happening? This can't be real, is my uncle really going to die?" Grief is a strange thing. We all feel different stages of it at different times. I was first hit with denial and anger. I denied it because I strongly believed that Jesus was going to heal him of the disease and I would never imagine him hurting himself like that. I was angry because I wished I was there to stop it from happening. I wish he would have called me to talk things through. My uncle and I were very close. We spent a lot of time together discovering the joy found in Jesus, selling kettle corn, cleaning his ten acre property, and eating delicious BBQ. I wasn't ready to let him go, but it was decided that the life support would be turned off the next day. As the doctor came in the room to turn off the machine, Greg's closest family and friends were in the room with him. We watched him breath his last breath at 5:55pm.

You don't just "move on" from something like this. I cried every day for weeks, and I can't think about him too long without crying still years after his death. To be honest with you, I felt so defeated when Greg died, and I didn't know how I was going to recover from it. I couldn't tell you how many times I had laid my hands on Greg to pray for his healing, but it's definitely in the hundreds. For six years, I put Greg on the top of my prayer list, asking Jesus to heal him of that terrible disease. I truly believed that God could do it too. In my ten years of being a Spirit-filled follower of Jesus, I have prayed for and witnessed thousands of people healed of all sorts of diseases and disabilities such as cancer, blind eyes, deaf ears, paralysis, and more. I always thought: "If Jesus did all that through my own hands, surely He can heal Greg too!" On a few occasions, myself and others would pray for him and he would suddenly stop shaking, and we thought that the disease was gone. But time after time the shaking and symptoms would return. It was always so hard to tell him the stories of people I had seen healed, and then watch him suffer and shake as I went on about how good God had been to someone else. After he died, my mind was full of unanswered questions. "Why did God heal all the other people but not my uncle… MY OWN UNCLE!" I was tempted to stop praying for the sick or disabled altogether after what had happened. But my God is greater. My God is good. He didn't take Greg. He didn't punish him with that terrible Parkinson's disease. Jesus is the giver of life, not the undertaker. What happened to my uncle, and my family was tragic, but as time past, the Lord began to reveal His goodness to me even in the midst of this pain. As I allowed Jesus to deal with my grief and pain, His great love overtook the plans of the enemy. The pain was so deep, and this wasn't the only time a loss like this has happened to me.

Even so, **His love is stronger than death**. His love renews and redeems us from loss. His love will make you laugh again. His love will deliver you from the harsh grips of grief. His love will make you dance and sing again. His love won't leave you in defeat, it won't leave you out to dry. His love proclaims a new day in your midst. You may feel surrounded by broken circumstances, but his love pulls you to the cross of Christ, where all things can be made new. You're not finished, your story doesn't stop here. You're path is looking brighter as you go, just look up and see it. He's here, with you through it all, and he will carry you till the end. *"And I am certain that God, who began the good work within you, will continue his work until it is finally finished on the day when Christ Jesus returns." (Philippians 1:6).*

His goodness has carried me to where I am today. After six deaths of close loved ones in the past four years, after losing a hero and father figure to a moral failure, after losing close friends, I remain confident in my friend Jesus.

A few years ago, I had the joy of leading a mission trip to South Africa with students from Bethel Church in Redding, California. On a particular night, I can remember the rush of excitement and faith as I arrived at a church service that my team was going to put on. The reason for my excitement was because the night before, I was preaching and asked if there were any blind people in the room. The whole church of around 150 people pointed over to a woman on the left side (I'll call her Mary). I asked Mary to come to the front so my team and I could pray for her and watch Jesus renew her sight. She was 100% blind! I shouted into the microphone, "God heals the blind, God opens the eyes of the blind, Jesus is here right now, I believe that He will open the eyes of this woman!" (Watch the actual video on Youtube by searching for my page: *jacobcoyne*). We put our hands on her head and began to pray with all the faith we had in us. After about 15 seconds of prayer... yes, seconds, Mary opened up her eyes and looked right at me! She was healed! The whole church went B-A-N-A-N-A-S after they witnessed this mighty work of God. We ended the service after this miracle. We couldn't stop celebrating Jesus!

Now let's get back to the following night at the next church service. Our team was ready for anything. Once you see God heal the blind, you have faith that any impossible situation can be solved. The pastor of the church heard about the miracle from the night before, so he introduced me to a blind boy who was about five years old. There was something in me that was so certain he would be healed and would be able to see that night. I made it my focus that night to pray only for the boy until he could see.

Well, as the hours went by, the service wrapped up and there wasn't any progress. He was still just as blind as when I met him. Letting him go that night was so hard for me. How could I see a woman healed the night before, and now a little boy has the same condition as she did but didn't receive the same solution? I had to walk away from that night trusting Jesus. It wasn't the boy's fault, and wasn't Jesus' fault either. I let this remain a mystery, but I also walked away from this experience with more fire in my heart to see Jesus get what he paid for when he died on the cross.

The questions you can ask yourself, God, and others, in these moments can either make your faith or break your faith. Even when we don't see God move the way we thought he would, we still have to make the choice to trust him. We can't allow our circumstances to dictate our theology. The Bible tells us to walk by faith, and not by sight. When what we are seeing doesn't align with what we are believing, then it's time to go back to the drawing board and spend time in the presence of Jesus. I've experienced many moments of hurt and pain in my life, and I'm assuming you have too. But if I allowed those hurts and those moments of disappointment to shape the way I see God, then God will look less and less like the one I read about in the Bible.

When things aren't going our way, it's time to cling to Jesus and ask Him to replace our doubts with His faith.

Come to him with your raw pain and brokenness, and watch what he can do with it. Today, I still trust Jesus and believe he is the great physician. Nothing is impossible with God *"Blessed are those who have not seen, and yet believe." (John 20:29 NIV)*

His life-giving Spirit will always conquer death.

"Where, O death, is your victory? Where, O death, is your sting?" (1 Corinthians 15:55)

Yet preaching the *Good News* is not something I can boast about. I am compelled by God to do it. How terrible for me if I didn't preach the *Good News*!

1 Corinthians 9:16

Chapter Four

THE

LAST

"But many who are first will be last, and many who are last will be first." (Matthew 19:30 NIV)

"But many who are the greatest now will be least important then, and those who seem least important now will be the greatest then." (Matthew 19:30 NLT)

On a scorching hot day in Redding, California, I was out and about with some friends filming a project for Bethel Church. As we began working in the downtown area, I noticed something strange across the street. Bottles were flying out of a dumpster over and over again! Now, I am a curious person, so I left my friends behind to see what was happening. I looked inside and there I found a dark haired, middle-aged man, wearing a tattered bright yellow polo and jeans. Confused, I looked at him and said, "Dude what are you doing in here!? Come out!" So the homeless man jumped and out introduced himself to me, "Hey there, I'm Donnie, I was just collecting some recycling so I can grab a good meal tonight." To the side of the trash can I saw three large bags of recyclable bottles and cans. "Donnie, I was wondering if anyone has ever told you how much Jesus loves you. I want you to know that he sees you today and celebrates you every day. I'd love to pray for you if that's fine with you." He looked shocked as I said this to him, as if he was being set up for a trap. Donnie then told me "Jacob, you really think Jesus is celebrating me today? Because it's my

50th birthday." I tried to hold back the tears as I realized this homeless man was alone, trying to earn enough money just to purchase a meal on his 50th birthday. I stopped and wondered how he got to where he was at in life. How many birthdays had Donnie spent alone?

I know that on the day he was born, someone looked at him with love in their eyes and said "What a beautiful baby boy." He was once celebrated by others, but now it's just him, and he had never known that Jesus was always right next to him in the trash, on the streets, in the homeless shelter, and in the cold and rainy winter.

Suddenly, I had an idea! A frozen yogurt shop was up the street so I shouted, "Donnie come with me! You can't have a birthday without ice cream! It's on me." As we walked together to the shop, tears streamed down his face, and now, down my own as well. We walked in and I told everyone in the store that Donnie turned 50 that day, and the employee said that he could get whatever he wanted for free. So Donnie poured in as much chocolate froyo as he could in one cup. Chocolate was dripping all over his hands, but he didn't care, it was his birthday! As we walked back to the dumpster that we first met at, my ten or so friends found us there. We all sang happy birthday to him and prayed for him and his back pain. As we all prayed, he felt the pain in his back subside and completely go away! As I said my goodbye to Donnie, he put down his trash and his messy chocolate frozen yogurt, knelt to his knees and began praying to Jesus. It was one of the most unforgettable moments of my life. I couldn't tell who was more impacted by the love of God, me or Donnie?

That night, my friend who witnessed all of this, Jason Chin, told me that he looked up the name Donnie, and it means "king." To me, this was so significant because I felt lead by Jesus to treat this homeless man like a king on that day. This divine encounter has changed the way I see Jesus and people forever. We aren't paupers and beggars in God's sight, we are kings and queens, we're his daughters and sons! Jesus wants to celebrate you, just like we celebrated Donnie that day. Sometimes life brings us to a place where we feel alone, isolated, invisible, and unlovable. You may even believe that you can end up in a dumpster looking for recyclable cans and no one would notice you or how you ended up there. Maybe it's been months since someone has told you that they love you. The truth is, millions of people in this world feel like Donnie did in the trash on his birthday. Believe me, I've been there many times.

But Jesus is outside of the dumpster you are in right now calling your name, anxiously waiting to celebrate you and shower you with his love and mercy. And if he needs to, he will even jump in there with you. He is the king of glory, and the king of the trash. He notices you. When we look in the mirror, we might see trash, but God sees his masterpiece.

*"But you are not like that, for you are a **chosen** people. You are **royal** priests, a **holy** nation, **God's very own possession**. As a result, you can show others the goodness of God, for he called you out of the darkness into his wonderful light. "Once you had no identity as a people; now **you are God's people**. Once you received no mercy; now you have received God's mercy." (1 Peter 2:10).*

Let that verse you just read sink in for a moment. Read it again, or pray and ask God to help you see yourself this way, the way he truly sees you. You're not trash, you're his most prized treasure. What did we have to do to earn this new identity as chosen, royal, and holy children of God? Nothing! We could never muster up enough good works and impressive feats to earn such a reward from a perfect God. This is the beauty of grace: Our identity is solely dependent on Jesus giving it to us. He earned our reward by his perfect life and his suffering on the cross for us and as us. We need to begin to realize God isn't look for our impressive talents and righteous deeds. He is looking for our "yes".

He's looking for us. He doesn't love you because of what you do, he loves you because of who you are. Jesus says this about us in his own words:

"The Kingdom of Heaven is like a treasure that a man discovered hidden in a field. In his excitement, he hid it again and sold everything he owned to get enough money to buy the field. "Again, the Kingdom of Heaven is like a merchant on the lookout for choice pearls. When he discovered a pearl of great value, he sold everything he owned and bought it!" (Matthew 13:44-46)

We are the treasure and the pearl that God found! When God "sold everything" to get a hold of us, he gave up Jesus. God had to give his most prized possession in order to win us back to Him again. *"For God so loved the world that He gave his only begotten Son so that whoever believes in Him would not perish but have everlasting life." (John 3:16).* Are you beginning to see your value to Jesus yet? You are worth everything that God gave up for you.

We are not the last thing on God's mind.

We are not an inconvenience.

We are loved by Him.

You Matter To Jesus

Do you often feel like you are just a face in a crowd or a number on a chart? Do you feel like you're the last choice in life's game of pick up basketball? In the system of our government, we are identified by our social security number. Even when we visit the doctor, or get our license renewed at the dreaded DMV, we are called by a queue number. If you feel depersonalized and dehumanized, as if you were faceless and nameless, that is exactly how the enemy wants you to feel — like you don't matter to God. Like you are very last on His list of people to love on. This is so far from the truth.

Listen, you matter to God! And what matters to you, matters to him. He calls you by your very name. He sees you right now and is in your midst as you are holding this book in your hands. He knows exactly what you are going through at this moment and where you are hurting on the inside. He delights in you and cares for you, and as W.M Paul Young states, "*He is especially fond of you.*" You are loved much more than you could ever know or imagine. (Ephesians 3:20).

He eagerly waits to do for you what he did long ago for a lonely and broken woman on a mountain in Samaria. The Bible says that *"He (Jesus) **needed** to go through Samaria to get from Judea to Galilee." (John 4:4)*. Now, any Jew of Jesus' time would have taken a different and longer route to avoid going through Samaria because they hated the Samaritans. Jews would refer to Samaritans as scum, rubbish, and the dogs of society.

"They were segregated from Jewish living. Here is why: The Samaritans were a group of people who lived in Samaria - an area north of Jerusalem. They were half-Jews and half-Gentiles. When Assyria captured the northern kingdom of Israel in 721 B.C. some were taken in captivity while others were left behind. The ones left behind intermarried with the Assyrians. Thus these people were neither fully Hebrews nor fully Gentiles. The Samaritans had their own unique copy of the first five books of Scripture as well as their own unique system of worship. At the time of Jesus the Jews and the Samaritans did not deal with one another. Jesus, however, ministered to the people of Samaria, preaching the good news to them." - Don Stewart

We know that Christ looks through a different lens than most of us. He walks in perfect love, and sees the heart, not the outward condition or appearance. Fully aware of the issues between the Jews and Samaritans, Jesus deliberately took the shorter, avoided route, just so He could stop by Samaria to have a divine appointment with a lonely Samaritan woman who had been searching for something in her life to satisfy her.

This particular woman had gone through five failed marriages and the man she was currently living with was not her husband. Clearly, something was off in her life. We can see that she had been carrying brokenness with her for quite some time at this point. She was likely looking for answers and fulfillment, and must have felt ashamed about her failed marriages and current lifestyle of cohabiting with another man.

Yet, in spite of all this, she mattered to Jesus! He needed to go to her to reveal true love to her. The only love that can break our heavy chains is the true love of Jesus. All alone, at noon, this woman hiked up to the city's well to fetch some water for the day. It was custom for the women of that time to hike to the wells together as a group. They also did this earlier in the morning to avoid the heat of the day. The

Samaritan woman likely traveled alone due to her status in the community. No woman wanted to associated with a promiscuous type like her. She was the last to travel up the mountain that day, but in doing so, this made her the first Samaritan to have a life changing encounter with the living God. Instead of fetching well water that day, she drank from the living water of Jesus. The Savior meets the Samaritan, and reveals to us that Jesus, the First and the Last, will come to the last and call them first. And indeed, after she met Jesus, the perfect Man, she was transformed. She was no longer ashamed, no longer alone, and no longer in chains. She was so touched by this love that she forgot to bring her jar of water down the mountain as she sprinted down to tell the other Samaritans about the Savior of all. She trotted down the mountain a new woman, and this new woman became the first preacher and evangelist to Samaria. Her testimony of Jesus caused many other broken and forgotten Samaritans from that town to hike back up the mountain to meet Jesus. He didn't withhold his love to any of them. No matter who we are or where we are at, his love is able to reach us and pull us out of our pits. (see John 4:28–29).

Jesus longs to meet you wherever you are at in life and and offer His grace to you. You do matter to Him. He cares about the very things that you care about. You may feel like you are in last place, like you are the last person Jesus wants to see or speak to, but never forget that he ***needed*** to go through Samaria just to speak to one woman who felt the same way. If Jesus offered her life, then why not you? He came to give you life and life more abundantly (see John 10:10). You are not just a face in a crowd or a number. No, he knows you by name and has true, everlasting love for you. And in spite of the mess that you might be in right now, he wants to meet your every need and make your life beautiful! Just as he needed to pass through Samaria to save this woman, he desperately longs to get to you. Allow him to come in, and make all things new.

For it is by grace you have been saved, through faith—and this is not from yourselves, it is the gift of God— not by works, so that no one can boast.

Ephesians 2:8-9

Chapter Five

THE

LITTLE

"Then Jesus said to his disciples, "Whoever wants to be my disciple must deny themselves and take up their cross and follow me. For whoever wants to save their life will lose it, but whoever loses their life for me will find it. What good will it be for someone to gain the whole world, yet forfeit their soul? Or what can anyone give in exchange for their soul?" (Matthew 16:24-26)

It is impossible for the champions and winners in the world's game of life to find purpose in following Jesus. When we believe the lie that our victories and blessings in life are the product of our own doing and muster, we have deceived ourselves. In order to fully sink into the grace of God, we must let go of our need to look great, creative, and excellent. There is nothing wrong with those things, but if we we make the pursuit of greatness and excellence an idol in our lives, we will miss Christ altogether. This is why it was so easy for the shepherds and children to come to Christ, and so difficult for politicians and Pharisees to make their way toward Him. Children carry innocence and awe. They depend on their parents to take care of them, and they are great at receiving gifts! You will rarely see a child turn a free gift away. This is the way of grace. Also, in the time of Jesus, shepherds were known for having the lowest ranking jobs, and were considered as the lowest class in Jewish society. But if you recall, of all people, shepherds were the ones who were invited by God himself to the birth of Christ. In the kingdom of God, the last, the lost, the least, the little and the lifeless are the ones that receive heaven's great prize. The champs and the winners all believe that salvation and grace can be earned, as if it were some sort of cosmic reward. Grace can never be earned, it is a free gift, and I praise Jesus for that truth. Jesus runs to the low and the losers because they realize their great need for a savior. We must come to our senses and realize that we are all in need of these things as well.

We are lost wanderers, nomads, looking for a place to call home. We are the prodigal sons and daughters.

We are the walking dead, waiting for life to wake us from our slumber.

We are the unqualified. The least likely choice when stacked up next to the rest of the bunch.

We are the last to receive the invitation to the party.

We are the little children that the Pharisees and disciples shoo away, because there are more mature, adult matters at hand.

Yet, we are the ones that Jesus runs to. We are the ones that Jesus adores. We are the ones that have a seat at the king's table. We are his. Jesus gladly takes what we are, so that we could become what he is.

He took our death on the cross and raised us back to life. His life. True life.

He took our lostness and prepared a place for us in heaven where we are forever found.

He left the safety and peace of His Father's kingdom to find us. You and me. We are his pearl of great price. We are the apple of his eye. We are chosen and beckoned to his side. We are his beloved

Why? Simply because. Because that is who Jesus is. He is love. We aren't loved because of our goodness, we are loved because of God's goodness. You will never be more or less loved by God than you are right now. The fullness of the Father's love is all around you, and he is at the door of your heart waiting to overwhelm you with it. We have nothing to give in return but ourselves, and that is all he desires.

Here is an excellent definition of the good news of grace from Paul Zahl:

"Grace is a love that seeks you out when you have nothing to give in return. Grace is love for you that has nothing to do with you. Grace is being loved when you are unlovable…. The cliché definition of grace is 'God's unconditional love.' It is a completely true cliché, for it is a good description of his grace. Let's go a little further, though. Grace is a love that has nothing to do with you, but has everything and only to do with the lover, or giver of that grace. It has nothing to do with weights and measures. Grace has nothing to do with my unique qualities or so-called 'gifts.' It has nothing to do with my past, present or future. It has nothing to do with my personality type. It reflects a decision on the part of the giver, the one who loves, in relation to the receiver, the one who is loved, that negates any qualifications the receiver may personally hold…. Grace is one-way love."

Children understand this love best. As adults we unlearn grace and begin to fall into the world's system of earning and reward. We lose the awe and wonder of grace. God calls us his children, not his employees.

Jesus said, *"Let the little children come to me, and do not hinder them, for the kingdom of heaven belongs to such as these." (Matthew 19:14).*

Grace doesn't make demands. It just gives. Religion demands, but grace supplies. And from our perspective, it always gives to the wrong person. We see this over and over again in the Gospels: Jesus is always giving to the wrong people—prostitutes, tax collectors, half-breeds. The most extravagant sinners of Jesus's day receive his warmest welcome. Grace doesn't make sense. It refuses to play it safe and lay it up. Grace is recklessly generous, uncomfortably extravagant. It refuses to keep score.

As the late Robert Capon put it, *"Grace works without requiring anything on our part. It's not expensive. It's not even cheap. It's free."*

It refuses to be controlled by our cultural standards of fairness. It defies logic. God's grace has absolutely nothing to do with earning, merit, or what we deserve. If it did, it wouldn't be grace. Grace is only grace when it's free. It is opposed to offering loans that need to be paid off. It doesn't expect a return on investments. Grace is unconditional acceptance given to an undeserving person by an extravagant giver. His name is Jesus.

This is the good news.

Examine the handiwork of grace in your own life for a moment. Odds are you have caught a glimpse of this grace at some point, and it made all the difference. Someone let you off the hook when you least expected or deserved it. A friend gave you the benefit of the doubt at a key moment. Your father was forgiving when you wrecked his sports car. Your teacher gave you an extension on your assignment, even though she knew you had been procrastinating. You let your nerves get the best of you and let your bad day out by saying something insensitive to your spouse, and instead of retaliating, she kept quiet and didn't hold it against you the next day. If you're married, go give your spouse a kiss and thank them for all the grace they give you every day, you know you need it! My wife is amazing for what she puts up with, as I'd consider myself an EGR kind of spouse… "Extra Grace Required."

Extravagant free grace has the incredible power to produce generosity, kindness, loyalty, and an abundance of love. Once grace catches you, you can't help it, you start living like Jesus! And yet, as beautifully lifesaving as grace can be, we love to resist it. By nature, we are suspicious of promises that seem too good to be true. We think there's a catch or a bait and switch to be discovered later on. We all hate opening those emails and letters that tell us what we've "already won." What's the catch? What's the fine print? What's in it for them?

Grace is a beautifully wrapped free gift, pure and simple. We might insist on trying to pay, but the balance has been settled and our money or cards are no good!. Even if we're able to accept Jesus' extravagant grace when it comes our way, like I've mentioned before, we have trouble when it reaches other people - especially those who've done us wrong. Grace offends our sense of justice by being both scandalous and unfair. We are uncomfortable because grace turns the tables on us, and relinquishes us of control. It forces us to rely on the goodness of another, and that is simply terrifying. We all have a hard time with dependence. So, in our human reliance, we try to domesticate the message of grace... after all, who could trust in or believe something so radically unbelievable?

The idea that there is an unconditional love that relieves the pressure, forgives our failures, and replaces our fear with faith seems too good to be true.

As we long for hope in a world of hype, the Gospel of Jesus Christ is the news we have been waiting for all our lives. Jesus came to liberate us from the hard knock life of having to make it on our own, from the demand to measure up. He came to free us from the heavy weight to get it all right, from the obligation to fix ourselves, find ourselves, and free ourselves. Jesus came to release us from the ugly need to be right, rewarded, regarded, and respected. Because Jesus came to set the captives free, life does not have to be a tireless effort to establish ourselves, justify ourselves, and validate ourselves.

Once this good news grips your heart, it changes everything. It frees you from having to be perfect. It frees you from having to hold it all together. In the place of exhaustion, you might even find energy. No, the Gospel of grace is not too good to be true. It is true! It's the truest truth in the all of the universe. God loves us no matter what we may or may not bring to the table.

There are no strings attached… No ifs, ands, or buts.

No qualifiers or conditions. No need for balance. Grace is the most dangerous, expectation-wrecking, smile-inducing, beautiful reality there is.

Grace is a bit like a roller coaster; it makes us scream in terror and laugh uncontrollably at the same time. But there aren't any seatbelts on this ride. We are not in the driver's seat, and we did not design the ride. We have to decide to just get on board. We laugh as the binding law of gravity is suspended, and we scream because it looks like we're going to blast off into space. Grace brings us back into contact with the children we once were and still are—children who loved to ride roller coasters, to smile and yell and throw our hands up in the air. Grace, in other words, is terrifyingly fun, and like any ride worth standing in line for, it is worth coming back to again and again. In fact, the good news of grace may be the only ride that never gets old, the only ride we never outgrow. Jesus and his grace are the source of inexhaustible hope and joy for an exhausted world.

Only good news.

Believe it, receive it, and don't turn back. It's yours for free, now freely give it away to all the lost, last, least, little, and lifeless souls around you. There is so much more for us, and and it's time we step into it… all of it. I pray this book goes from our heads straight to our hearts, that we would be transformed to live the life in Christ that we were all destined to live. Don't let circumstances and lies keep you from His goodness. The good news is enough, Jesus is enough, and He always will be.

Cheers.

ABOUT THE AUTHOR

Jacob Coyne is a husband, dad, pastor, and Bible teacher.

Ever since he was radically saved in high school, Jacob has been boldly sharing the life changing message of Jesus both locally and globally. His life inspires those around him to let go of the past and to live wholeheartedly for Jesus. Thousands have said yes to Jesus through Jacob's various preaching, teaching, and missions opportunities around the globe.

Jacob and his wife Mariah live in Washington State with their two beautiful daughters, and wild boston terrier.

Ways to follow & contact Jacob:

Instagram: @jacobcoyne
Facebook: facebook/jacobcoyne
Website: jacobcoyne.com
Email: jacobcoynespeaks@gmail.com

Made in the USA
Coppell, TX
08 July 2020